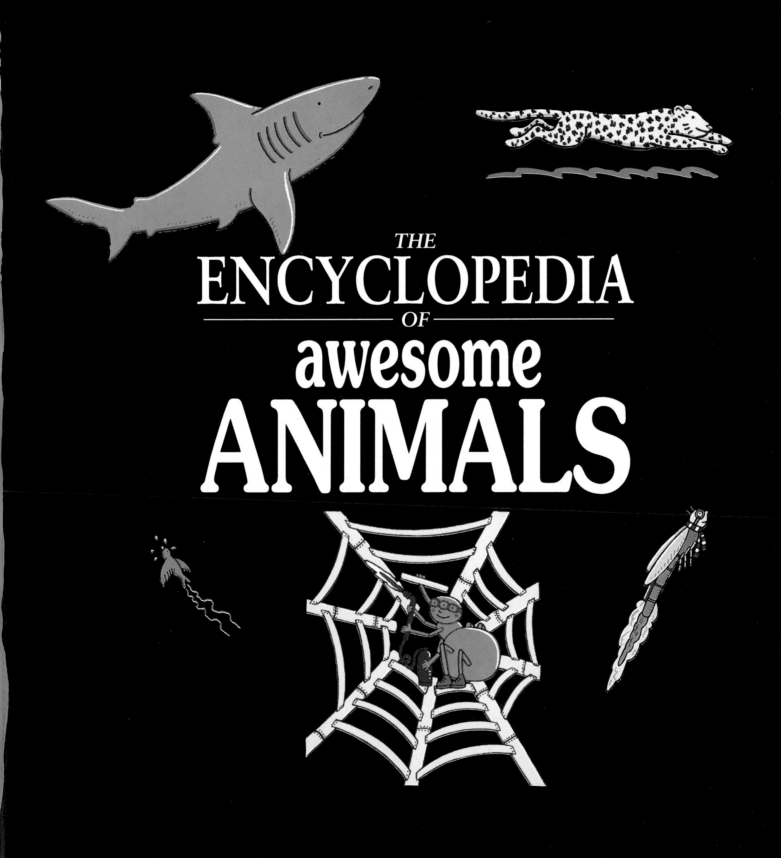

THE
ENCYCLOPEDIA
OF
awesome
ANIMALS

© Aladdin Books Ltd 1998

Produced by

Aladdin Books Ltd

28 Percy Street

London W1P 0LD

ISBN 0-7613-0781-8

First published in the United States in 1998 by

Copper Beech Books,

an imprint of

The Millbrook Press

2 Old New Milford Road

Brookfield, Connecticut 06804

Concept, editorial, and design by

David West Children's Books

Designers: Robert Perry and Flick Killerby

Printed in Belgium

CIP data for this publication is
available at the Library of Congress

THE
ENCYCLOPEDIA
— OF —
awesome
ANIMALS

COPPER BEECH BOOKS
BROOKFIELD, CONNECTICUT

Contents

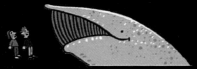

Introduction

Discover for yourself the most amazing facts about the most awesome animals – from the dim and distant past of prehistory, when dinosaurs roamed the earth, to the present day when new and improved beasts fly, swim, and hunt for food. Chapter by chapter this book will keep you informed about the world of natural history, from crocodiles, alligators, and sharks silently hunting in the deep to the flight of insects, birds, and even snakes! You will also read about the prides, pods, and troops of lions, whales, and apes. From the biggest beast that ever lived, swimming in the ocean deep, to the tiniest spider, which you can barely see, the *Encyclopedia of Awesome Animals* will show you the world.

 Watch for this symbol that means there is a fun project for you to try.

Is it true or is it false? Watch for this symbol and try to answer the question before reading on for the answer.

Chapter One

sharks

by
Claire
Llewellyn

Illustrated by Jo Moore
and Darren Harvey

Introduction

Discover for yourself amazing facts about sharks – what they eat, how they have babies, who their enemies are, and more.

Did *you* know that some sharks are older than dinosaurs? ... sharks are the biggest fish? ... some sharks glow in the dark? ... some have heads like hammers? ... if sharks stop swimming they sink? ... sharks keep losing their teeth? ... sharks feed in a frenzy? ... sharks can smell blood over a half mile away? ... some fish hitch rides on sharks? ... some baby sharks grow inside mermaids' purses? ... people are sharks' worst enemies?

I didn't know that

sharks are older than dinosaurs. Sharks' ancestors lived about 200 million years before the dinosaurs. Some were giants and had spines on their heads.

SEARCH & FIND
Can you find five trilobites?
FIND & SEARCH

Few sharks turned into *fossils*, but their teeth did! This tooth (left) measures 12 inches and belonged to a monster shark called megalodon. A great white shark's tooth is half this size.

Cladoselache lived about 350 million years ago, and measured over 6 feet from teeth to tail. The shark's mouth was at the tip of its snout, not tucked underneath as in most sharks today.

Cladoselache

This fossil of a shark, called stethocanthus, shows that it had thorny spines. Fossils of sharks are rare because their skeletons are made of *cartilage*, which rots away before it can fossilize.

! Port Jackson sharks still have spines, just like their ancestors did.

To see how big a whale shark really is, try making one in the park or on the beach. Using a yardstick as a guide, measure out its length, and then fill in the outline with pebbles or twigs.

The basking shark is the world's second largest fish. It swims with its mouth open, to catch microscopic sea creatures.

I didn't know that

sharks are the biggest fish.

The whale shark measures up to 42 feet, and is the largest fish in the sea. This gentle giant feeds peacefully, filtering tiny plants and animals from the water.

Whale shark

SEARCH & FIND
Can you find three divers?
FIND & SEARCH

The dwarf shark is just 6 inches long, not much bigger than a goldfish. In fact, half of all known sharks measure less than three feet.

Whale sharks are so gentle that divers can ride on them.

Megamouth shark

I didn't know that

some sharks glow in the dark.
Some sharks that live in the deep, dark
parts of the ocean make their own
light. The jaws of a megamouth
shark give out a silvery glow. This
probably attracts tasty shrimps.

SEARCH & FIND
FIND & SEARCH
Can you find six jellyfish?

The frilled shark has elongated eyes to see in the murky depths.

The goblin shark (above right) lives at the bottom of the sea. Its long, sensitive snout helps it to find any prey nearby.

Sensitive snout

Lantern sharks (left) glow in the water thanks to a luminous slime on their skin. Experts think the coloring may help sharks to attract their prey or keep their place in a *shoal*.

The cookie-cutter shark gets its name from its curious bite. When the shark attacks another animal, it leaves a wound that is perfectly round – just like a cookie.

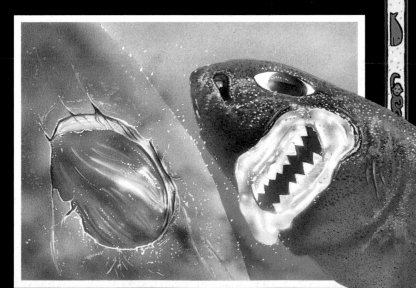

The wobbegong is a strange-looking shark with speckled skin and tassels that make it look like a rock or seaweed. The fish makes use of this *camouflage* by hiding on the ocean floor and snapping up fish.

Stingray

Gill slits

Sharks are related to rays (right). Both groups of fish have gill slits instead of flaps, and skeletons of cartilage rather than bone.

True or false?
Some sharks have wings.

Answer: **True**
The angel shark's large fins (left) are just like wings. It uses them to glide along the ocean floor as it searches for *crustaceans* and fish.

Angel sharks are called monkfish as they seem to be wearing a hood.

I didn't know that

some sharks have heads like hammers. The hammerhead shark has a T-shaped head just like the top of a hammer. As the shark swims, it swings its head from side to side so that its eyes have an all-around view.

Great hammerhead shark

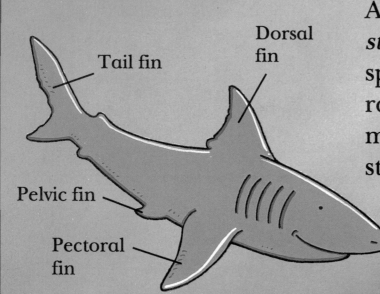

Tail fin

Dorsal fin

Pelvic fin

Pectoral fin

A shark's body is sleek, *streamlined,* and built for speed. Its fins are large and rather stiff, and help it to move forward, stay upright, steer, and stop.

Like all fish, sharks have gills to take in oxygen from water. As water flows over the gills, tiny blood vessels absorb the oxygen and carry it around the body.

Mako shark

16

I didn't know that

if sharks stop swimming, they sink. Most fish have an air-filled bag called a swim bladder inside them, which helps to keep them afloat in the sea. Sharks don't have swim bladders. To avoid sinking, most sharks have to swim all the time – just like treading water.

 True or false?
Some sharks sleep in caves.

Answer: **True**
The whitetip reef shark is a sleepy fish. At night, it cruises sluggishly around coral reefs, and spends the day sleeping on the ocean floor. It often hides away in caves to avoid being spotted and disturbed.

 The pectoral fins give a shark lift, just like the wings on a plane.

I didn't know that

sharks keep losing their teeth. Sharks often lose their teeth as they attack their prey, so new teeth constantly grow inside their mouths. Slowly the new teeth form and move outward to replace the older ones.

SEARCH & FIND & FIND SEARCH & FIND SEARCH &

Can you find five teeth?

Sand tiger shark

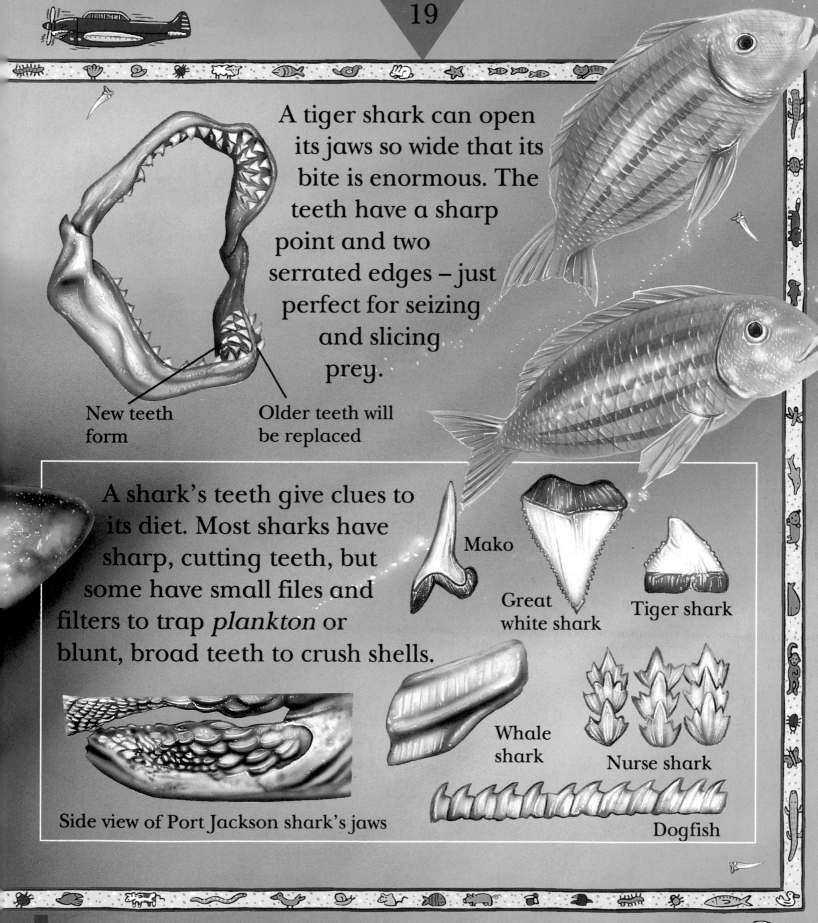

A tiger shark can open its jaws so wide that its bite is enormous. The teeth have a sharp point and two serrated edges – just perfect for seizing and slicing prey.

New teeth form

Older teeth will be replaced

A shark's teeth give clues to its diet. Most sharks have sharp, cutting teeth, but some have small files and filters to trap *plankton* or blunt, broad teeth to crush shells.

Mako

Great white shark

Tiger shark

Whale shark

Nurse shark

Side view of Port Jackson shark's jaws

Dogfish

Sharks can't chew their food. They have to swallow it in large chunks.

Sharks eat all kinds of foods: seagulls, seals, turtles, crustaceans, and plankton. They rarely eat people. They don't like the taste of human flesh!

Blue sharks

I didn't know that sharks feed in a frenzy. When sharks feed, others may join in. As they snap at the food they get excited by the blood and movement in the water. They can bite or kill each other during this "feeding frenzy."

Found in the stomachs of sharks: a mustard jar, plastic bag, beer cans...

A shark's jaws lie a long way under its pointed snout. As the fish lunges to bite, it lifts its nose out of the way, and swings its jaws forward. Then it rolls up its eyes inside its head to protect them during the attack.

 True or false?
Some sharks attack with their tail.

Answer: **True**
The thresher shark has a long tail, which it lashes in the water like a whip. Scientists think that this either stuns its prey or herds fish into a tightly-knit group, which the thresher shark then attacks.

Sharks have a lateral line on each side of their body, which picks up vibrations in the sea. It helps sharks to feel the things that are moving around them, such as a seal or a fish.

Oceanic whitetip shark

SEARCH & FIND
Can you find the other fish?
FIND & SEARCH

A shark's body is covered, not with scales, but with toothlike bumps called denticles. These are very coarse, and feel rough if they're stroked the wrong way.

I didn't know that

sharks can smell blood over a half mile away. Sharks have a keen sense of smell. As water streams past their nostrils, they pick up messages in the sea around them. Some sharks can sniff the blood of a wounded animal over a half mile away, and race toward it.

Sharks have tiny *organs* on their snout that can pick up electrical signals. Since every creature in the sea produces some kind of electricity, these organs help sharks to hunt them down.

❗ Shark skin was once used on sword handles to give a good grip.

I didn't know that

some fish hitch rides on sharks. Remoras are small fish with a sucker pad on their heads. They use it to cling on to sharks. As they ride, they help by eating *parasites* on the sharks' skin.

Sucker pad

Like surfers, remoras ride on the waves made by sharks.

Small, agile pilot fish often swim alongside a shark. They probably feel safe near their large companion, and can also feed on scraps of its food.

Zebra shark

SEARCH & FIND
Can you find ten remoras?
FIND & SEARCH

Copepods are crustaceans that stick to a shark's fins and feed on it. They may even cling to a shark's eyes, so that it can hardly see.

I didn't know that

some baby sharks grow inside mermaids' purses. Some sharks lay their eggs in leathery cases called mermaids' purses. Inside the purses, the eggs grow into baby sharks. They eat the yolk and hatch ten months later.

SEARCH & FIND & SEARCH & FIND &
Can you find the mother shark?

Swell shark embryos

Three months old

Seven months old

While some sharks hatch out of eggs, most develop inside their mother's body. They feed either on egg yolk or on food in their mother's blood, and are later born live, like *mammals*.

A baby lemon shark emerges from its mother.

Next time you're on the beach, try to find a mermaid's purse. The dogfish is a common shark and its dry, black egg cases are often washed up on the shore.

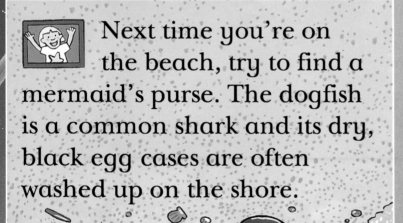

Many sharks try to protect their eggs. The horn shark wedges her spiral-shaped egg case into a crack in a rock. Other egg cases have long tendrils that cling to plants.

Horn shark egg

A whale shark's egg is the size of a football.

I didn't know that

people are sharks' worst enemies.

Large, meat-eating sharks have no enemies in the sea. But people kill them for sport, and for their meat, skin, and oil. Also, many sharks get trapped in our fishing nets, and drown.

Great white shark

True or false?

Sharks are blood-thirsty killers.

Answer: **False**

This is a myth that movies, such as *Jaws*, have helped to spread. Most sharks leave people alone. Scientists believe that attacks only happen when a shark mistakes a swimmer for a seal or other kind of prey.

Surfer

Seal

Bull shark

Sharks die so that people can make soup from their fins, jewelry from their teeth, and medicines and lipsticks from their oil. Yet all these things can be made using other materials.

Some people catch sharks for sport, and treat their bodies as trophies. Every year, the number of large sharks in the sea falls.

Shark liver oil pills

Jewelry

Shark fin soup

Cosmetics

Sharks seem to attack more men than women.

Chapter Two

big cats

by Claire Llewellyn

Illustrated by Peter Barrett, Jonathan Pointer, and Jo Moore

Introduction

Discover for yourself amazing facts about big cats – from snow leopards in the Himalayas to jaguars in South America and more.

Did *you* know that lions are related to pet cats? ... big cats are the top predators? ... a tiger hunts by itself? ... a cheetah runs as fast as a car? ... some cats wear jungle camouflage? ... only some big cats can roar? ... some cats wear snowshoes?

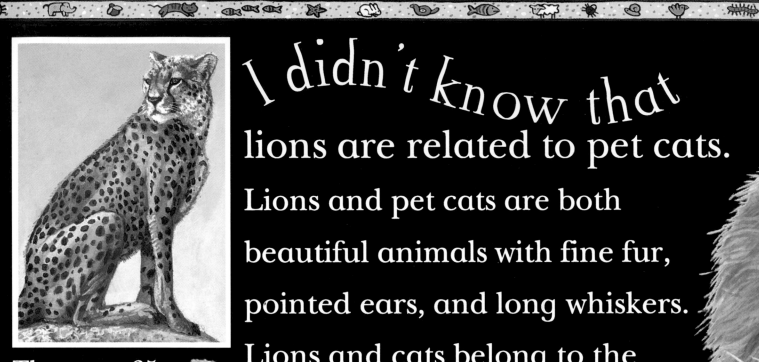

I didn't know that

lions are related to pet cats.

Lions and pet cats are both beautiful animals with fine fur, pointed ears, and long whiskers. Lions and cats belong to the same animal family, the Felidae, and behave in many similar ways.

Domestic cat

There are 35 kinds of cats. They fit into four groups: great cats, small cats, clouded leopards, and cheetahs (above). The cheetah has its own group because it runs faster and can't pull in its claws.

The domestic cat is the only cat to mix happily with humans.

Male lion

A saber-toothed tiger stabbed its prey with its long teeth, then waited for it to die. They lived over 5 million years ago but died out at the end of the *Ice Age*.

I didn't know that

big cats are the top *predators*. The big cats hunt many kinds of animals, such as wild pigs, zebra, and deer, but are not hunted themselves. This makes them the top predator in the *food chain*.

A cat's long tongue is covered by small, horny spikes called papillae. These help the animal to scrape off the last bits of meat and lick the bones clean.

Tigers enjoy eating crabs, frogs, and fish.

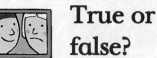

A lion's strong, bony skull anchors powerful muscles that deliver a deadly bite. The jaws are heavy, with long, pointed teeth to stab the prey. Jagged side teeth slice its flesh into chewable portions.

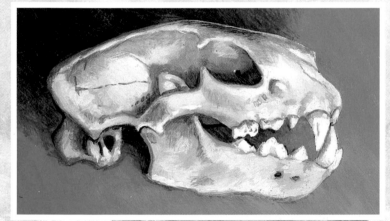

True or false?

Lions have to eat every day.

Answer: **False**

Lions kill large animals and eat a huge amount of meat at a single feed. They can go several days before eating again.

35

A leopard often drags its kill up into a tree, where it will be safe from wild dogs, hyenas, and other hungry animals. The food lasts the leopard several days.

I didn't know that

a tiger hunts by itself.

A tiger stalks its prey silently, creeping closer and closer before going for the kill. All cats' eyes face forward on the front of the head. This helps them to judge distances accurately.

True or false?

Cats' eyes light up the road.

Answer: **True**

The glass road markers that reflect car headlights are known as cats' eyes.

Cats can see in the dark. Their large eyes collect as much of the dim light as possible, and then boost it with the *tapetum*, a special shiny layer at the back of the eye.

Cats have sharp, hooked claws that pin down and cut their prey. The claws can be pulled up inside the paws, so that cats can move silently on super-soft pads.

I didn't know that

a cheetah runs as fast as a car. It is the world's fastest land animal. Over short distances, it can reach speeds of 60 mph. Its long claws work like an athlete's running spikes, and give it a better grip.

A falling cat will turn in the air so it always lands feet first. Its flexible legs and spine "give" on impact so the cat is usually unhurt, even if it falls a long way.

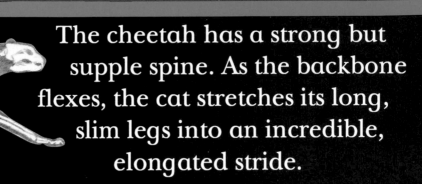

The cheetah has a strong but supple spine. As the backbone flexes, the cat stretches its long, slim legs into an incredible, elongated stride.

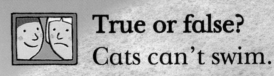

True or false?
Cats can't swim.

Answer: **False**

Tigers are good swimmers. They often go into rivers and streams to cool off or chase their prey.

SEARCH & FIND & SEARCH & FIND & SEARCH

Can you find the capybara?

True or false?
Panthers don't have spots.

Answer: **False**
Panthers have a black coat, but in bright light you can still see their spots.

A panther's black coat hides it in the dark rainforest.

I didn't know that

some cats wear jungle camouflage. Jaguars live in the hot, steamy rainforests of South America. Their spotted coat makes perfect camouflage. It blends in with the forest's dappled light and hides them as they hunt.

The tiger (above) lives in grasslands and forests. Its stripes help to hide it in the tall grass, and the changing forest light.

Turn yourself into a beautiful animal. Find some face paint, and copy the markings of your favorite cat on to your own face.

I didn't know that

only some big cats can roar. Small cats can purr, but they can't roar. Lions, tigers, leopards, and jaguars can all roar. Cheetahs can't. Big cats often roar at dawn and dusk to warn other cats to stay away from their territory.

A lion's roar is very loud – you can hear it up to five miles away.

Like many cats, a cheetah marks its *territory* with scent. It backs up to trees and sprays them with urine. It's the cats' way of telling strangers to "Keep Out."

Try to make a pet cat purr. All you have to do is stroke it. Cats purr when they are contented, and females purr as their kittens feed.

**True
or false?**
Lions use their
tails as flags.

Answer: **True**
When it is hunting in long
grass, a lion holds up its tufted
tail for other lions to follow.

True or false?
Tigers live only in
tropical lands.

Answer: **False**

The Siberian tiger lives in icy Siberia
in eastern Russia. The animal is larger
than tropical tigers and has a thick,
shaggy coat of fur.

The puma (left) lives in the
mountains of North America,
where winters are often severe.
The cat's large, thick paws help
it to balance on icy slopes as it
bounds after snowshoe hares.
It also hunts elk and sheep.

! Snow leopards leap across very wide ravines.

Lynx (right) spend the winter in pine forests, sheltering from the worst of the weather. Although they are one of the smaller cats, they have very big, furry feet.

Cats wear two coats: a layer of soft wool close to their skin for warmth and a top layer of coarse hair that keeps out moisture.

I didn't know that

some cats wear snowshoes. The rare snow leopard lives high in the Himalayan mountains. During the winter it grows thick fur on its feet to broaden them, and prevent them from sinking in the snow.

Chapter Three
crocodiles
& alligators

by Kate
Petty

Illustrated by
James Field and Jo Moore

Introduction

Discover for yourself amazing facts about crocodiles and alligators – the differences between them, where they live, what they eat, how they have babies, and more.

Did *you* know that crocodiles are survivors of the dinosaur age? ... you can tell an alligator by its teeth? ... crocodiles yawn to keep cool? ... crocodilians pretend to be floating logs? ... alligators can leap into the air? ... some crocodiles eat only twice a year? ... crocodiles blow bubbles? ... crocodile eggs squeak? ... crocodiles carry their babies in pouches? ... some crocodiles swim in the sea? ... some alligators sleep through winter?

I didn't know that

crocodiles are survivors from the dinosaur age. A crocodile looked much the same in the dinosaur age as today. Crocodiles belong to a *reptile* family that wasn't wiped out 65 million years ago.

Can you find the big dinosaur?

Sarcosuchus

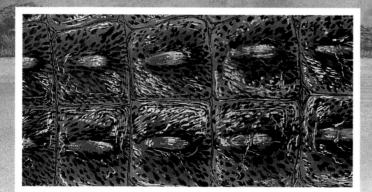

A crocodile's armor-plated skin is made up of horny scales called scutes, with extra protection from the bony plates just below the surface.

Crocodiles belong to the *crocodilian* family. So do their American cousins, the alligators (there is also a rare Chinese alligator), and so do caimans, and the gavial.

Crocodile

Gavial

Alligator

Caiman

Some *prehistoric* crocodiles were giants, some up to 40 feet long. They would almost certainly have preyed on other reptiles, including small dinosaurs.

! Early prehistoric crocodiles were as small as lizards.

True or false?
Crocodiles and alligators never meet.

Answer: **False**
The American crocodile is rare and the American alligator is flourishing, but both are found in the swamps of Florida.

Saltwater crocodile

Crocodiles are found in tropical areas, including Florida. Most of them live in inland waters. Crocodiles are the biggest crocodilians.

Most alligators (apart from the Chinese one) are found in North and South America. They have squarer jaws than crocodiles.

American alligator

Our baby teeth are replaced once by grown-up teeth, but a crocodile's teeth can be replaced 40 times as they wear down.

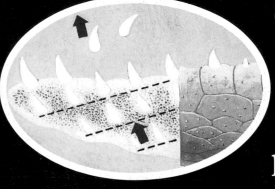

I didn't know that

you can tell an alligator by its teeth. Only the top teeth can be seen when the alligator's jaw is closed. A crocodile, on the other hand, shows some of its lower teeth as well.

The name "alligator" comes from "el lagarto," Spanish for "lizard."

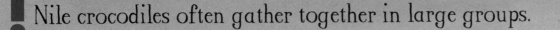

A little bird, the Egyptian plover, is safe within the jaws of a Nile crocodile. It picks out parasites and leeches, doing the crocodile a favor.

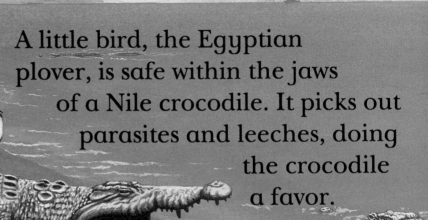

Nile crocodile

I didn't know that

crocodiles yawn to keep cool. Crocodiles are *cold-blooded*. They bask in the sun for warmth or cool off in the water. Cool air on the thinner skin inside their mouths stops them from overheating.

SEARCH & FIND ♦ FIND SEARCH ♦ FIND SEARCH ♦

Can you find five floating crocodiles?

Reptiles never stop growing throughout their lives. Young crocodiles grow 12in a year. Imagine if that happened to you!

The saltwater crocodile from Southeast Asia is a giant, the biggest of all living reptiles. The record is held by an individual that measured 27ft and weighed two tons. The smallest crocodile is the rare African dwarf that measures only 5ft.

In the movie *Peter Pan*, a crocodile swallowed a clock.

I didn't know that

crocodilians pretend to be floating logs. They lie submerged and completely still in the water. Their eyes and nostrils are on top of their heads so they can see and breathe as they lie silently in wait for their prey.

Can you find the baby caiman?

SEARCH & FIND
FIND & SEARCH

Black caiman

Some crocodiles stay underwater for an hour. Special flaps close off their nostrils, throats, and ears. A special, clear eyelid protects the eyes.

A crocodile's back feet are webbed, like a frog's. Webbed feet help it to steer and maneuver quickly in the water if it needs to.

Fish-eating crocodiles, like the Australian freshwater crocodile (right), often have long, thin snouts, good for catching fish, and a streamlined body.

! Caimans are preyed on by anaconda snakes.

I didn't know that

alligators can leap into the air from the water if their lunch is high up. Smaller crocodiles even climb trees to catch insects and snails. They all move fast, running or swimming, to launch a surprise attack on their prey.

American alligator

The gavial catches several fish at once with a sideways swipe of its head and grips them in its sharp teeth.

True or false?
Some crocodiles are muggers.

Answer: **True**

One type of Indian crocodile is called a mugger. It is a man-eater and its main victims are women washing clothes and children playing on the riverbank.

I didn't know that

some crocodiles eat only twice a year. If a crocodile catches a large animal it will eat it all at once and digest it over a long period of time. It lunges at its prey, aiming to knock it into the water.

Rocks have been found in the stomachs of crocodiles. They swallow them to help grind up their food.

A crocodile's teeth are designed for gripping, not for chewing. It tears the meat off in chunks and swallows them whole.

The struggle between crocodile and prey can be a tug of war.

Crocodiles have very strong jaws that lock on to their prey.

Nile crocodiles help each other when they feed. One holds the prey down while the other feeds off it. Groups of young Nile crocodiles cooperate to catch fish.

Wildebeest

The gavial's name comes from a word for "pot" and describes the shape of the lump on the male's nose (left). The "pot" works as an amplifier for his mating call.

Nile crocodile

In the mating season, male crocodiles behave strangely! They fight to decide who is strongest. The American crocodile (below) snaps and splashes the water with his jaws to keep others out of his territory.

Crocodiles can communicate using smell.

Courting couples put on *displays*, rubbing heads or lying alongside each other with their mouths open. This female saltwater crocodile raises her head out of the water to show that she wants to mate.

I didn't know that

crocodiles blow bubbles. A male Nile crocodile sometimes lowers his head into the water and blows bubbles through his nostrils. He also growls and lashes his tail as a threat to other males.

When a baby crocodile hatches it has a sharp point on its snout called an egg tooth. It needs this to break its way out of the hard-shelled egg where it has lain tightly curled.

Crocodile parents guard the nest against raiders such as birds or baboons. The parents of these eggs were caught off-guard by two thieving monitor lizards working together.

Saltwater crocodile hatchlings

I didn't know that

crocodile eggs squeak.

The *hatchlings* let their mother know when they are ready to come out. High-pitched noises from inside the shells bring the mother to scrape off the nest coverings that kept them warm.

A mother crocodile makes a nest on land where her eggs can be kept safe and warm. She makes it in the same place every year. She lays the eggs at night, a few at a time, and covers them.

SEARCH & FIND SEARCH & FIND &

Can you find the kingfisher?

I didn't know that

crocodiles carry their babies in pouches. A mother crocodile has a pouch in the bottom of her mouth. As soon as the babies hatch she picks them up one by one and carefully takes them to the water.

Mother and father watch over the young crocodiles in a "nursery" at the waterside. The babies catch their own small fish and crabs while the parents keep watch.

Mugger crocodile

Crocodile and alligator babies cannot look after themselves very well. A young alligator may hitch a ride on its mother's back.

I didn't know that

some crocodiles swim in the sea. The estuarine – or saltwater – crocodile from Southeast Asia and Australia is the biggest of all crocodiles and the only one to swim in the sea. It lives in estuaries along the coast.

Can you find five turtles?

Australian aboriginal art often contains pictures of crocodiles. This is because according to their ancient beliefs the spirits of the dead live on in crocodiles.

66

Saltwater crocodile

True or false?

Crocodiles always eat meat.

Answer: **False**

The rare African dwarf crocodile lives in swamps and slow rivers. It eats fish, frogs, and also fruit!

The ancient Egyptian god of water, Sobek, was in the shape of a crocodile. This is how he looked in paintings. Use modeling clay to make your own Sobek pendant. Don't forget to make a hole for the chain, shoelace, string, or ribbon.

The so-called "false" gavial is in fact a crocodile.

I didn't know that

some alligators sleep through winter.
Alligators dig holes and passages underground
where they can escape the heat and
cold. Chinese alligators and the most
northerly American alligators
hibernate in these tunnels.

SEARCH & FIND
SEARCH & FIND

Can
you find
the snake?

There are only 600 of these Chinese alligators left living in the wild. They are protected by law but poachers still kill them for their skins and meat.

The dwarf caiman from the Amazon basin is one of the smallest alligators. Caimans live in South America. They have armor on their backs and their bellies.

There have been reports of alligators using sewers as their tunnels.

Chapter Four

apes & monkeys

by
Claire
Llewellyn

Illustrated by
Jo Moore and Chris Shields

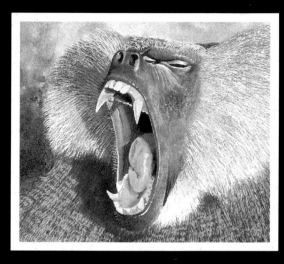

Introduction

Discover for yourself amazing facts about monkeys and apes – their differences, what they eat, how they communicate and show friendship, who their enemies are, and more.

Did *you* know that apes are different from monkeys? ... some monkeys live in large groups? ...some monkeys wear makeup? ... chimps have learned to use tools? ... eagles kill monkeys? ... some gorillas have silver fur? ... a monkey is the noisiest land animal?

I didn't know that

apes are different from monkeys. They are larger and can stand upright on their back feet. Apes include orangutans, chimpanzees, gorillas, and gibbons. Apes do not have monkeys' useful tails.

SEARCH & FIND Can you find four monkeys and two apes? FIND & SEARCH

Mangabey

Ring-tailed lemur

Monkeys and apes belong to a group of mammals called *primates*. Most primates live in the trees. They are clever with forward-facing eyes that help them to judge distances well. Bushbabies and lemurs are also primates.

Lowland gorilla

True or false?

Humans are primates.

Answer: **True**

Humans belong to the same family as apes and monkeys, but are not directly related. Scientists who study ancient fossils think that humans and apes shared a common ancestor about 10 million years ago.

! Apes have faces that are almost human.

I didn't know that

some monkeys live in large groups. Baboons live on open grasslands in large groups called troops. Males lead the troops and take turns acting as guards on the lookout for cheetahs and lions.

Apes and monkeys groom one another. It creates a bond between group members, and helps to keep them all friendly. It also keeps them clean!

SEARCH & FIND

Can you find the hiding lion?

FIND & SEARCH

True or false?
Some apes live all alone.

Answer: **True**
Orangutans live deep in the rainforests of Southeast Asia. Each animal stays in its own part of the forest, well away from its neighbors. The females live in small family groups with just a baby or two.

In a group of chimpanzees, the biggest, oldest, and cleverest chimps become more important than the others. Male chimps often threaten each other to try and improve their ranking.

Savanna baboons

Gibbons live in small groups, just mom, dad, and the kids.

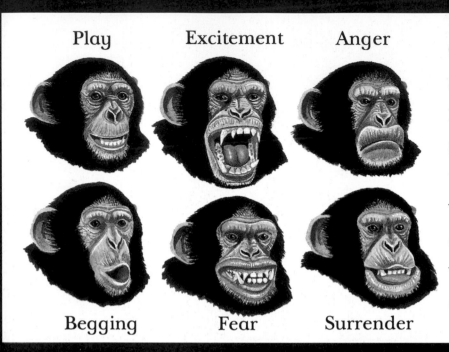

Play Excitement Anger

Begging Fear Surrender

Chimpanzees pull all sorts of faces and can make many different sounds. This helps them to keep in touch with each other, avoid arguments, and to warn one another of danger.

 True or false?
A female monkey blushes with her bottom.

Answer: **True**
From time to time, a female monkey's sitting pads become large and bright pink. This is a clear signal to the males that she is ready to mate.

Apes' and monkeys' faces are bare to show their expressions.

Mandrill

I didn't know that

some monkeys wear makeup. Mandrills live in the dark African rainforest. The male's brightly-colored face shows up well in the forest and helps him to attract a mate.

Turn yourself into a handsome mandrill. Find a set of face paints and a mirror and copy the monkey's markings. Draw the outline of the design before you color it in.

I didn't know that

chimps use tools.

Chimpanzees are clever inventors. They have learned to peel long, thin twigs and then use them as fishing rods to "fish" out tasty termites from nests and mounds.

An ape's hand is like a human's. The thumb swivels around to touch each of the fingertips, allowing the owner to pick things up and handle them with care.

Chimpanzee

78

True or false?
Apes can learn a language.

Answer: **True**

Apes have intelligent minds. Over the years, scientists have studied the animals and have taught them to communicate with symbols and signs. One gorilla learned to "say" whole sentences in sign language. Other apes have learned more than 100 different symbols.

Monkeys learn from one another. It is said that in Japan, a young macaque found a potato on the beach and washed off the sand in the sea. Other macaques copied her; now they all wash their food.

! Apes will never speak because they can't make the necessary sounds.

I didn't know that

eagles kill monkeys. Monkeys need to watch out for harpy eagles. These sharp-eyed hunters fly silently over the forest. They grab monkeys from the branches and crush them in their powerful claws.

Harpy eagle

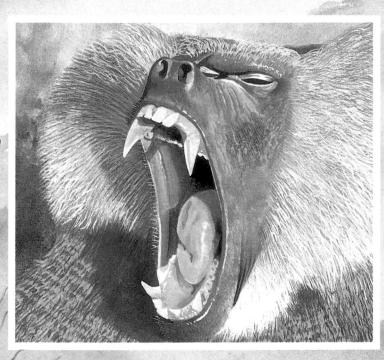

True or false?
Some monkeys have fangs.

Answer: **True**
Baboons have a pair of very long, pointed teeth (left). Males snarl and bare their fangs to frighten leopards, lions, and other hunters that sometimes threaten the group.

A male gorilla scares off its enemies by standing up tall, baring its teeth, roaring loudly, and beating its chest with its hands (right).

Capuchin monkey

I didn't know that

some gorillas have silver fur. Adult male gorillas are called silverbacks because the hair on their back turns silver-gray. A large silverback protects the troop and decides where it sleeps and feeds.

Mountain gorilla

SEARCH & FIND & FIND & SEARCH

Can you find the elephant?

Gorillas are the world's largest primates. They have massive skulls, sturdy legs, and powerful muscles. Yet, gorillas are gentle vegetarians. They eat shoots, roots, leaves, fruit, and fungi.

 True or false?
Gorillas make nests in the trees.

Answer: **True**
Each evening, gorillas make nests of branches and leaves in the trees or on the ground. They make nests at midday, too, for a lunchtime nap.

! ... but weighs three to four times more.

The owl monkey lives in South America and is the world's only *nocturnal* monkey. Its large eyes help it to see in the dark.

Owl monkey

The monkey with the longest nose is the male proboscis monkey from South-east Asia. When he's excited, his nose turns red, which helps him to attract a mate.

The world's most famous primate appeared in the movie *King Kong*, made in the 1930s (left). The movie is about a giant gorilla and is set in New York City.

In ancient Egypt, Hamadryas baboons were sacred.

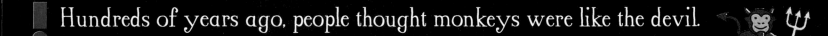

Howler monkey

I didn't know that

a monkey is the noisiest land animal. South American howler monkeys make a deafening noise that can be heard 26 miles away. The loud howls are made by the hollow shape of the monkeys' lower jaw.

Chapter Five

whales & sea mammals

by Claire
Llewellyn

Illustrated by
Jo Moore, Darren Harvey,
Robin Carter, and Steve Roberts

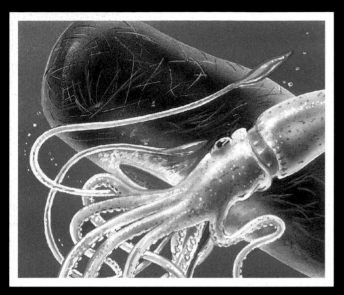

Introduction

Discover for yourself amazing facts about whales and dolphins – what they eat, how loud the humpback whale's call can be, how they have babies, who their worst enemies are, and more.

Did *you* know that whales are mammals that breathe air? ... a whale is the largest animal ever to live on Earth? ... whales can hold their breath? ... whales are acrobats? ... some whales have no teeth? ... killer whales hunt in packs? ... there can be thousands of dolphins in a school? ... some whales travel 12,000 miles a year? ... whales sing? ... whales need midwives?

I didn't know that

whales are mammals.

Just like you, me, cows, horses, cats, dogs, and all the other mammals, a whale is *warm-blooded*, breathes air, and drinks milk from its mother when it's a baby.

SEARCH & FIND

Can you find the fishy imposter?

& FIND & SEARCH

Beluga whale

Great right whale

Killer whale

Gray whale

Porpoise

Sperm whale

Amazon river dolphin

Narwhal

Bottlenose dolphin

Blue whale

Humpback whale

Whales don't need fur to keep them warm. A thick layer of *blubber* keeps them warm in the cold seas.

Vestigial limb

From being a land mammal, a whale's body has adapted to a sea-going life. Its front legs became flippers and its back legs disappeared altogether. If you look at its skeleton you can just see the remains (vestiges) of them.

! Inuits eat whale blubber to protect them from the cold.

True or false?
A blue whale's heart is four times the size of a man.

Answer: **True**
At least! It weighs 900 lbs. An average man weighs about 220 lbs.

The blue whale is sometimes known as a sulfur-bottomed whale. On deep dives it picks up tiny algae that stick to it, making it glow in the dark.

Blue whale

SEARCH & FIND

FIND & SEARCH

Can you find the penguin?

I didn't know that

a whale is the largest animal ever to live on Earth. The blue whale is four times the size of the largest dinosaur and 25 times the size of a large elephant. An animal this big couldn't live on land – but in the sea the water can support its enormous weight.

Brachiosaurus

African elephant

The tongue of a blue whale is the same weight as a hippopotamus!

I didn't know that

whales can hold their breath. They have to! Although they are mammals that have lungs and breathe air, most whales spend a lot of time underwater. They come to the surface to breathe.

Blowhole

Lung

The *blowhole* on top of a whale's head is its nostril. The whale blows out air in a high spout before taking deep breaths and going under again.

Gray whale

A whale's lungs would be crushed by its weight on land.

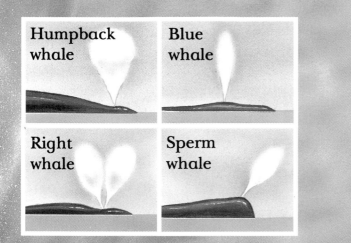

Humpback whale

Blue whale

Right whale

Sperm whale

True or false?
You can tell a whale by its spout, or blow.

Answer: **True**
A whale's spout is a cloud of vapor, made when the whale's warm, moist breath hits the cooler air. The pictures show spouts from different whales. Nineteenth-century whale-hunters would spot the spouts from a distance and could often tell from them what sort of whales were nearby.

Sperm whales hold the whale record for diving with dives of 9,000ft, sometimes lasting over an hour. Their heads contain a waxy substance called spermaceti, which might help them to survive the pressure at such great depths.

I didn't know that

whales are acrobats. Like this 50-foot humpback, many whales leap out of the water as they surface. They sometimes twist or somersault before crashing back into the water. This is called breaching.

Humpback whale

Dolphin

Fish

Fish waggle their tails from side to side to move forward. A whale has strong muscles to move its tail up and down. It uses its flippers for stability and steering.

True or false?
Dolphins leap out of the water to frighten the fish.

Answer: **True**
Imagine the commotion caused in the water by a breaching whale or dolphin! The frightened fish crowd together into tight groups, which makes it easier for the dolphins to catch them.

Dolphins, including killer whales (the largest dolphins), perform in marine parks. People are fascinated by their agility and intelligence. It's sad that the dolphins are captive but the audiences learn that they should be protected in the wild.

An individual whale can be identified by the shape of its tail

I didn't know that

some whales have no teeth.

There are toothed whales and *baleen* whales. A baleen whale has several hundred whiskery sheets of horn, called "whalebone," hanging from the roof of its mouth to catch food.

The biggest whales feed on tiny, shrimplike krill. In one day, a blue whale might trap over 4 million.

Can you find the polar bear?

Great right whale

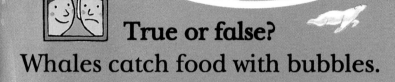

True or false?
Whales catch food with bubbles.

Answer: **True**
A whale can round up a shoal of krill by blowing bubbles as it spirals up from below them. The krill are spun into the center of the ring of bubbles where the whale can snap them up in one mouthful.

The whalebone corsets worn by fashionable Edwardian women were reinforced with strips of whalebone (baleen). Today, plastic would be used instead – but corsets have gone out of fashion!

Baleen whales may have evolved from insect-eating mammals.

I didn't know that

killer whales hunt in packs.

Killer whale

Killer whales, or Orcas, are large black-and-white dolphins. They live in groups called *pods* and hunt together. They eat fish, squid, seabirds, seals, and even other dolphins and whales.

The narwhal is a toothed whale with only two teeth. In the male, one tooth is a spiraled, nine-foot-long tusk. Narwhals use their tusks to duel with each other and to stir up fish from the seabed.

Harp seal

Sperm whales feed on giant squid deep in the ocean (right). The 50-foot-long squid aren't caught without a fight — many sperm whales have battle scars to prove it.

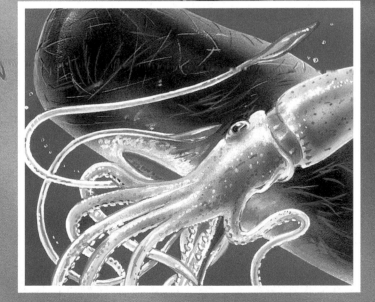

The killer whale in the movie *Free Willy* had a plastic stunt double.

True or false?
Whales are found only in the sea.

Answer: **False**
Dolphins are small toothed whales, and five species of them live in the rivers of South America, India, Pakistan, and China. Some Amazon river dolphins (left) live 2,000 miles away from the sea.

Porpoises are the smallest members of the whale and dolphin family. They are not "beaked" like dolphins. The way they jump through the water is called "porpoising," even when dolphins do it!

Dolphins will help an injured animal reach the surface to breathe.

SEARCH & FIND
Can you find the breaching whale?
FIND & SEARCH

I didn't know that

there can be thousands of dolphins in one *school*. Common dolphins gather in huge groups where there are plenty of fish to eat. Sometimes 2,000 of them will work together to herd and feed on shoals of fish.

The U.S. Navy uses dolphin intelligence! The one below is trained to locate and pick up torpedoes from the seabed. Others detect submarines and guard harbor gates.

Common dolphin

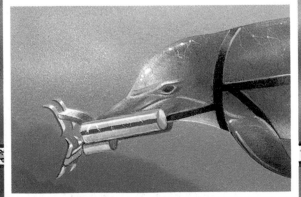

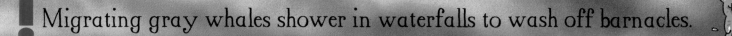

Gray whale

I didn't know that

some whales travel over 12,000 miles a year. Californian gray whales swim over 6,000 miles from Alaska to Mexico every winter to breed. They swim back for the summer when food is plentiful.

SEARCH & FIND & FIND SEARCH & FIND

Can you find the killer whale fin?

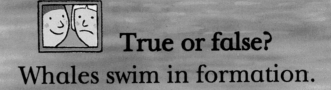

True or false?
Whales swim in formation.

Answer: **True**
Lots of whales, particularly dolphins, swim in formation. Herds of belugas *migrate* in formation as they file through the pack ice. From above you can see the formation (left) as they follow their food south.

Whales can become stranded if a beach slopes suddenly and they are left without enough water to support them. Their friends swim to their aid and then they too become stranded.

A gray whale mother will be aggressive in defense of her calf.

I didn't know that

whales can sing,

communicating across many miles of sea. Each one has a distinctive and recognizable song. The songs are made up of rumbles, clicks, and whistles. They are noisiest during the breeding season.

Arctic sailors used to call belugas "sea canaries" (above) because of the loud whistles and bell-like calls they made.

Humpback whales are famous for their songs. Each year they have a new sequence of notes. They will play around with the sounds of this sequence for hours on end.

The humpback's song can be heard 100 miles away!

The humpback whale's song can be as loud as a plane taking off.

Humpback whale

Sound waves from dolphin

Echo from fish

 Hunting dolphins use echolocation. They make a noise and wait for the sound waves to bounce back. Sound waves work like water waves. To see how they work, put a small cup in a sink of water with a dripping faucet. Waves from the drip bounce off the cup.

I didn't know that

whales need midwives. Like all newborn mammals, a baby whale needs to take its first breath as soon as it is born. A "midwife" whale helps the mother to push her newborn to the surface for air.

Humpback whale

 True or false?

A baby blue whale drinks 150 gallons of milk a day.

Answer: **True**

It doubles its weight in its first week and feeds from its mother for seven months, until it is 50 ft long.

When they are courting, whales often play together. The male swims alongside the female, cuffing her or stroking her tenderly with his head. Humpbacks leap out of the water together when they are mating.

Male dolphins show off to females (below) with high-speed chases and fights. They bite and snap at each other, but they hardly ever die from their wounds.

Male right whales perform a courtship dance.

Chapter Six
snakes

by
Claire
Llewellyn

Illustrated by
Francis Phillips, Ian
Thompson, David Wood,
Rob Shone, & Jo Moore

Introduction

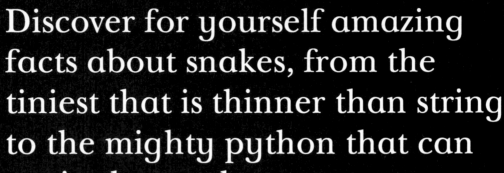

Discover for yourself amazing facts about snakes, from the tiniest that is thinner than string to the mighty python that can polish off an entire leopard at one sitting...

Did *you* know that snakes have scales? ... snakes lay eggs? ... some snakes move sideways? ... a snake smells with its tongue? ... snakes have fangs? ... some snakes spit poison? ... snakes have elastic jaws? ... pythons can live on one meal a year? ... some snakes have rattles? ... some snakes live in the sea? ... some snakes can fly?

I didn't know that

snakes have scales. Like all reptiles, snakes have dry, scaly skins made of a tough material like fingernails. The scales are watertight. They keep moisture in so the snake won't dry out in the heat.

Close-up of scales

Reticulated python

Try to find out the true facts about snakes. Touch one, and you'll discover that its skin is not slimy, but warm and dry. Also, far from being a danger, many snakes need our protection.

There are about 2,500 different kinds of snakes.

Snakes have never been very popular. Many people are frightened of them. In the Bible story, it is a snake that tempts Eve to disobey God and eat the forbidden apple.

Agama lizard

Galapagos tortoise

True or false?
Snakes are related to crocodiles.

Answer: **True**

Snakes and crocodiles both belong to the reptile family. It's a large family with about 6,500 different members. They're split into four main groups: lizards and snakes, crocodiles, turtles, and tuatara (related to the extinct dinosaurs).

Nile crocodile

SEARCH & FIND & FIND & SEARCH &

Can you find the lizard?

I didn't know that

snakes lay eggs. Most snakes lay soft, leathery eggs that they bury somewhere on land – in a hole in the sand or under a pile of rotting leaves. The eggs soon hatch into baby snakes.

Racer

Although most snakes lay eggs, some, such as vipers, are born live.

Baby snakes have a sharp tooth on their top jaw. They use this to cut their way out of their egg. Soon after they hatch, the egg tooth drops off.

 True or false? Snakes keep losing their skins.

Answer: **True**

As it grows, a snake's scaly skin becomes too small for its body. Every few months it sheds a paper-thin outer layer, which peels off like a long sock. Underneath, there's a shiny new skin in a larger size.

Egg tooth

King snake

I didn't know that

some snakes move sideways.

Desert snakes move over the sand in their own special way. They make a coil in their body, and throw it across the ground. This is called sidewinding.

True or false?
Snakes are warm-blooded.

Answer: **False**
Snakes are cold-blooded. They are not cold to touch, but their bodies are the same temperature as the air around them.

Sidewinder

A snake's backbone has hundreds of bones, like the links in a chain. Muscles pull the bones, helping the snake to move quickly – even without legs!

Ribs

Backbone

Skull

 Make a twisty, slithery snake from plastic yogurt cups. Join the cups together with paper fasteners, then add an extra cup for the head. Add a forked tongue.

Saw-scaled viper

The jumping viper can leap 3 feet up into the air.

True or false?
Snakes can see in the dark.

Answer: **False**
Even with poor eyesight some
snakes can hunt in the dark.
This is because they have
holes in their heads called pits,
which feel the warmth of any animal nearby.

Heat-sensing pit

Green tree viper

Snakes have no eyelids
and cannot blink. Each
eye is protected by a
see-through scale, giving
it a glassy stare.

 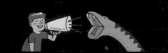

Jacobson's organ

I didn't know that

a snake smells with its tongue.

A snake's forked tongue picks up chemical messages from the air and the ground. These "tell" the snake whether a meal, an enemy, or a mate is near.

A special part of the snake's body makes sense of all these chemical messages. It is called the Jacobson's organ and lies in the roof of the snake's mouth, within easy reach of its flickering tongue.

Carpet python

117

I didn't know that

snakes have fangs. Poisonous snakes have long, hollow teeth called fangs. When snakes strike their prey, they sink their fangs into the animal and inject it with deadly poison. When the snake eats its prey it is not affected by the poison.

Fang

Gaboon viper

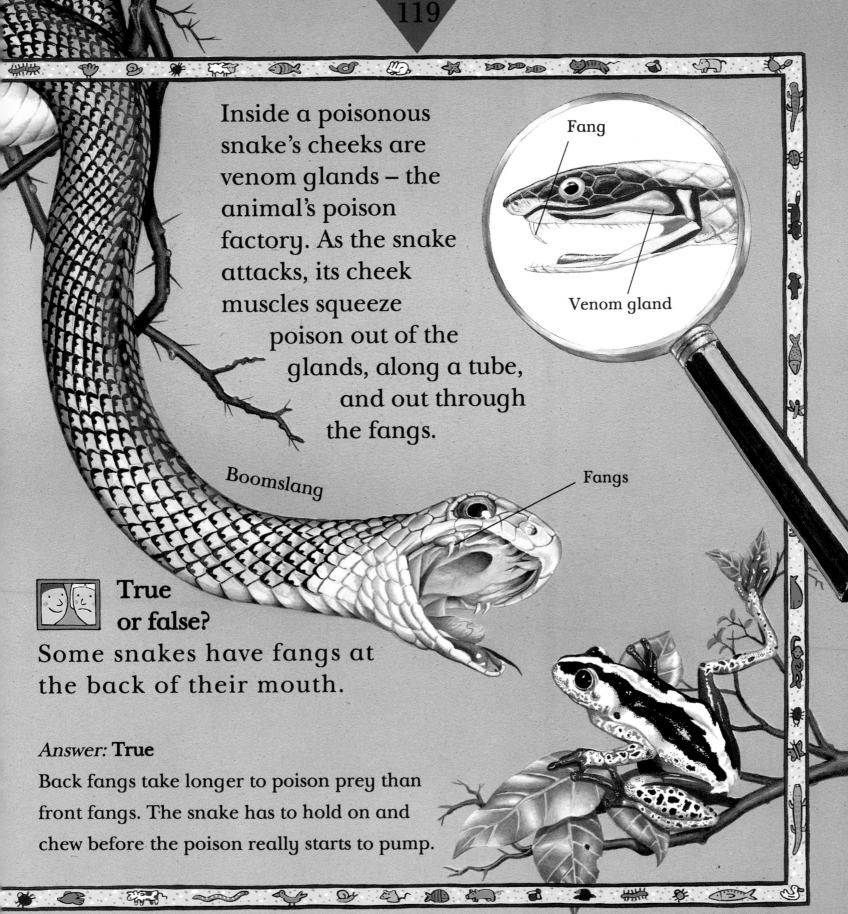

Inside a poisonous snake's cheeks are venom glands – the animal's poison factory. As the snake attacks, its cheek muscles squeeze poison out of the glands, along a tube, and out through the fangs.

Fang

Venom gland

Boomslang

Fangs

True or false?
Some snakes have fangs at the back of their mouth.

Answer: **True**
Back fangs take longer to poison prey than front fangs. The snake has to hold on and chew before the poison really starts to pump.

! Fangs are something like the hypodermic needles used by nurses.

I didn't know that

some snakes spit poison.

A threatened cobra will spray poison in its enemy's face. The poison causes burning or blindness if it hits the eyes.

Snakes are a symbol of healing. This is because people once thought that snakes could live forever, becoming young again each time they shed their skins.

Snake venom is "milked" to make medicine for snake bites.

Cleopatra was Queen of Egypt over 2,000 years ago. When Egypt was conquered by the Romans, she decided to kill herself. The story goes that she grasped a snake called an asp and died of its poisonous bite.

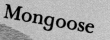

Mongoose

The British writer, Rudyard Kipling, wrote a story called *Rikki-tikki-tavi*, about a mongoose that saves a family from a cobra. Mongooses are fast and fierce, and are snakes' natural enemies.

This vine snake has caught a lizard.

True or false?
There are no vegetarian snakes.

Answer: **True**
All snakes eat some kind of meat. Many of them have a varied diet, feeding on insects, worms, fish, frogs, lizards, birds, and deer. People with pet snakes often feed them live mice!

Some snakes have no teeth, so they swallow eggs whole. Such large mouthfuls could choke them, but the snakes push their *windpipe* forward and so keep their airway clear.

Windpipe

Snakes' jaws are joined at the sides by a bony hinge. This "unhooks" during a meal, allowing the mouth to gape wide open. The bottom jaw is made in two parts that can separate.

Bony hinge

This stretchy material is called a *ligament*.

I didn't know that snakes have elastic jaws.

Snakes can swallow meals that are bigger than themselves. Their mouths open very wide because their skin is stretchy, and the bones in the jaws and skull can pull apart.

Egg-eating snake

! It can take a snake as long as several hours to swallow a meal.

I didn't know that

pythons can live on one meal a year. Pythons kill their prey by squeezing it until it stops breathing. These huge snakes are strong enough to kill a leopard – and may not need to eat another meal for a whole year.

SEARCH & FIND & FIND & SEARCH

Can you find the mouse?

True or false?
Snakes can hypnotize
their prey.

Answer: **False**

No snakes can hypnotize their
prey. But in the film of
Rudyard Kipling's *Jungle
Book*, a giant python called
Kaa tries to hypnotize
animals with his swirling,
colorful eyes. He hopes to put
them in a trance and kill them –
but he never actually succeeds!

Indian python

The mighty anaconda hunts
caimans in the rivers of the South
American rainforest. The snake
lies in wait low in the water and
then pounces on its prey – and
hugs it in its coils until it dies.

! The emerald tree boa feeds on birds in tropical rainforests.

I didn't know that

some snakes have rattles. When a rattlesnake feels threatened, it quickly shakes its horny tail. This makes a dry, buzzing noise, which frightens enemies away – just like a personal alarm.

When a stink snake is frightened, it raises its tail and makes a rotten smell that lasts for hours. The enemy runs away – fast!

Most snakes avoid a fight. They prefer to slither away.

Coral snake

Milk snake

Some snakes fool their enemies by pretending to be more dangerous than they are. The milk snake is harmless, but it has the same skin coloring as the deadly coral snake – a disguise that must often save its life.

Rattlesnake

True or false?
Some snakes dodge danger by pretending to be dead.

Answer: **True**
When an enemy appears, the grass snake (below) lies on its back with its tongue sticking out. It looks very dead! Because most meat-eaters prefer their meals fresh, the grass snake will be left alone.

I didn't know that

some snakes live in the sea.

There are about 50 kinds of sea snakes. Some of them live near the shore, but others spend all their time out at sea, diving and coming up for air.

Horned viper

SEARCH & FIND
Can you find ten clown fish?
FIND & SEARCH

Many snakes live in the desert. The horned desert viper hides from the midday sun by wriggling under the sand. It comes out to hunt at night.

Sea snakes have a flat tail that they use as a paddle.

Snakes in tropical forests hunt frogs, lizards, and birds. Some forest snakes are green and hang from the branches like vines. Others have patterned skin, which hides them among the foliage on the forest floor.

Green mamba

Banded sea snake

 True or false?
There are no snakes at all in Ireland.

Answer: **True**
People say that a Christian bishop, called Saint Patrick, believed all snakes were evil and banished them from the country. Saint Patrick lived over 1,600 years ago – but the snakes have never returned.

I didn't know that

some snakes can fly. The flying snake lives in the forests of Southeast Asia. To move from one tree to another, it raises its ribs, flattens its body, and glides smoothly through the air.

Flying snake

Thread snakes are the world's smallest snakes. Some of them are only 4 inches long, and are as thin as the lead in a pencil.

SEARCH & FIND
Can you find ten thread snakes?
FIND & SEARCH

Watch out for the African black mamba. It's the fastest land snake!

True or false?
Snakes live longer than people.

Answer: **False**

The oldest snake ever recorded was a boa constrictor called Popeye. Popeye lived in a zoo, where he was comfortable, safe, and well-fed. He was 40 years old when he died.

Boa constrictor

The heaviest snake in the world is the anaconda. The biggest anacondas can weigh more than 300 pounds. This is as much as two people.

Chapter Seven
spiders

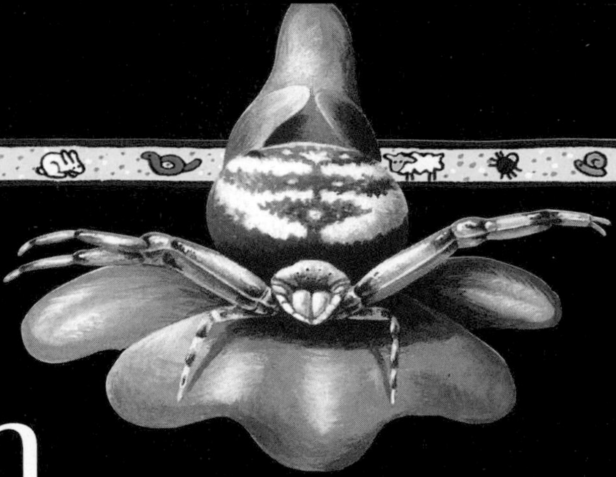

by Claire Llewellyn

Illustrated by

Myke Taylor &

Jo Moore

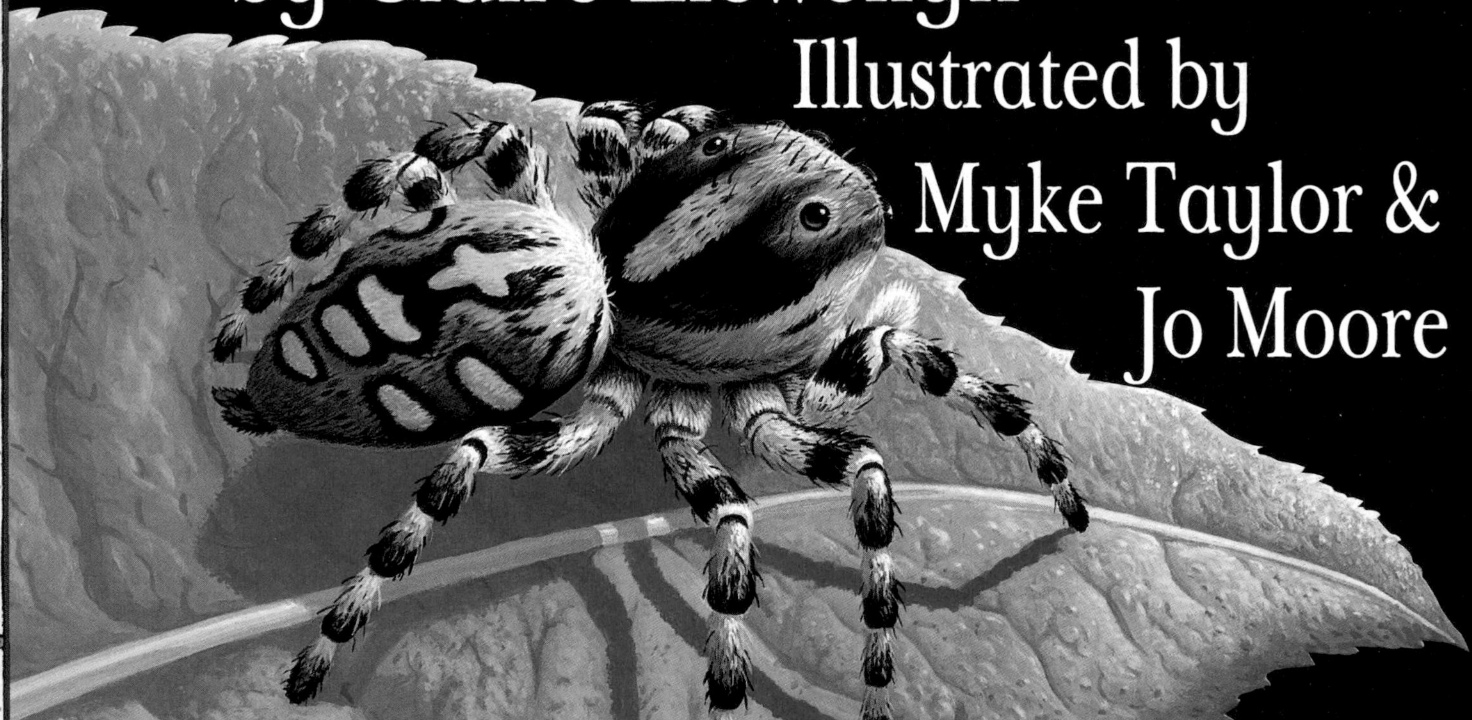

Introduction

Discover for yourself amazing facts about spiders and other arachnids, how they catch their food, what they eat, where they live, and how they defend themselves.

Did *you* know that spiders have eight legs? ... most spiders have eight eyes? ... some spiders jump through trapdoors? ... spiders have fangs? ... some spiders dance when they're courting? ... wasps attack spiders? ... some spiders are bigger than this page?

I didn't know that

spiders have eight legs. Spiders have four pairs of legs. So do scorpions, harvestmen, mites, and all the other members of the *arachnid* family. This makes arachnids different from *insects*, which have six legs.

SEARCH & FIND
Can you find the insect?
FIND & SEARCH

Red mite

Emperor scorpion

Wolf spider

A Greek myth tells of a girl called Arachne, who could spin so well that the goddess Athene was jealous, and turned her into a spider. Poor Arachne – now she could only spin webs!

Sun spider

Grasshopper

It's not easy being a spider! Stand back to back with three friends, link your arms, and try walking across the room. Eight legs need a lot of control!

Harvestman

Whip scorpion

Many insects can fly, but arachnids can't.

Spiders sometimes lose a leg when they shed their skin.

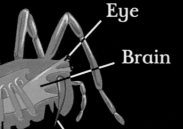

Heart

Liver

Silk glands

Ovary

Book lungs

Intestine

Fang

Eye

Brain

A spider's body is two halves, joined at the waist. The front has the brain, eyes, jaws, and legs. The back has the heart and organs for digestion, reproduction, and breathing.

True or false?

A spider has no bones.

Answer: **True**

Although it has no bones a spider has an *exoskeleton*. This is a hard suit of armor which protects its body, but doesn't grow. As the spider gets bigger, it bursts at the seams and sheds its skin. Underneath, there's a new exoskeleton in a larger size.

The shed skin, or cast, of the tarantula

I didn't know that

most spiders have eight eyes. These are on the front of their head. In spite of this, many of them can't see very well. They feel their way around with their legs.

Most spiders are soft and easy to eat, but the spiny-backed spider (above) has sharp spines that would stick in a bird's throat.

Indian ornamental tarantula

A spider sheds its skin about ten times as it grows.

I didn't know that

some spiders jump through trapdoors. Trapdoor spiders dig a burrow in the ground, cover it with a trapdoor, and hide inside. Then they pounce on any creature that passes.

SEARCH & FIND

Can you find five ants?

FIND & SEARCH

Giant millipede

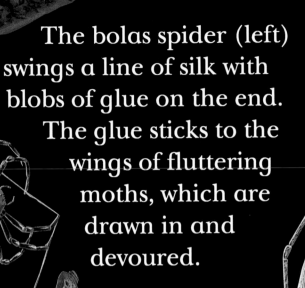

The bolas spider (left) swings a line of silk with blobs of glue on the end. The glue sticks to the wings of fluttering moths, which are drawn in and devoured.

The net-casting spider (right) spins a net then hangs head-down on a thread, holding the net and waiting. When an insect walks by, the spider scoops it up.

The bolas spider is named after the bolas, a South American lasso.

I didn't know that

spiders have fangs. Like snakes, spiders use poison to defend themselves and kill their prey. A spider jabs its fangs into its victim and holds on while the poison pumps into the prey.

SEARCH & FIND & SEARCH & FIND
Can you find the lucky bug?

Wandering spider

A spider can't break down food inside its body like we can. Instead, it injects each meal with juices, which change it into soup. Then the spider sucks it all up.

Most spiders' fangs are like pincers that move sideways toward each other to bite. Bird-eating spiders have long fangs that point straight down. They thrust them into their prey to bite.

Fangs

Bird-eating spider's fangs

In Taranto, Italy, 600 years ago, the people suffered from poisonous spider bites. They danced for days, hoping to flush out the poison. The town has given its name to the tarantella dance – and to the tarantula spider!

A spider bite always leaves two little holes in the skin.

A male web spider introduces himself to a female by plucking the threads of her web. He taps out a signal, which brings her running to meet him.

True or false?
A female black widow spider eats her mate.

Answer: **True**

Female black widow spiders are larger and fiercer than the males. After mating, a male needs to make a quick getaway, or the female will eat him up.

Male black widow

Female black widow

Some male spiders give dead flies to the females as presents.

SEARCH & FIND The red mark on the black widow spider. FIND & SEARCH

I didn't know that

some spiders dance when they're courting. Before trying to mate with a female, the male jumping spider dances and prances, waving his colorful legs. The female is dangerous, and may need soothing. This dance tells her he's a friend, not a foe.

Male jumping spider

Female jumping spider

I didn't know that

wasps attack spiders. The female tarantula hawk wasp feeds her babies tarantulas. She attacks, stings, and paralyzes these huge spiders, then drags them into a hole and lays an egg on them.

SEARCH & FIND
Can you find five wasps?
FIND & SEARCH

Tarantula hawk wasp

Cactus wren

Collared lizard

Desert tarantula

Spiders are tasty, and
have many enemies,
such as mammals, birds,
lizards, beetles, scorpions –
and even other spiders!

Many farmers kill pests by
spraying their crops with
chemicals. The sprays kill
spiders, too. This is a shame
because spiders eat many pests,
and are really the farmer's friend.

! A golden-wheeling spider escapes by cartwheeling down sand dunes.

Patu marplesi

I didn't know that

some spiders are bigger than this page. The world's biggest spider is the goliath bird-eating spider, which grows up to 11 inches wide. The world's smallest spider, *Patu marplesi*, is so small that you could fit ten of them on the end of your pencil.

The most charming, intelligent spider is Charlotte in the book *Charlotte's Web* by E. B. White. Charlotte lives in a barn, and saves the life of Wilbur, her good friend the pig.

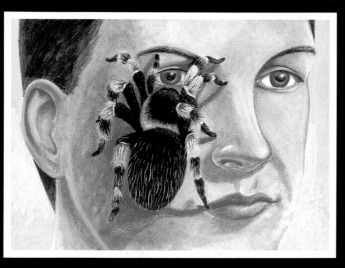

People who are scared stiff of spiders suffer from a fear known as arachnophobia. They should avoid the horror film *Arachnophobia* (above) – it's definitely not one for them!

Goliath bird-eating spider

One of the world's most poisonous spiders is the funnel-web spider from Australia. Its venom is deadly to some animals, such as primates and creepy-crawlies. But to many other mammals, like cats and dogs, it's harmless!

Chapter Eight

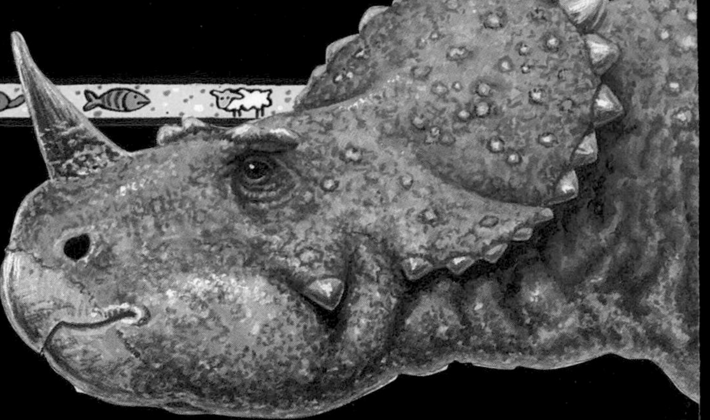

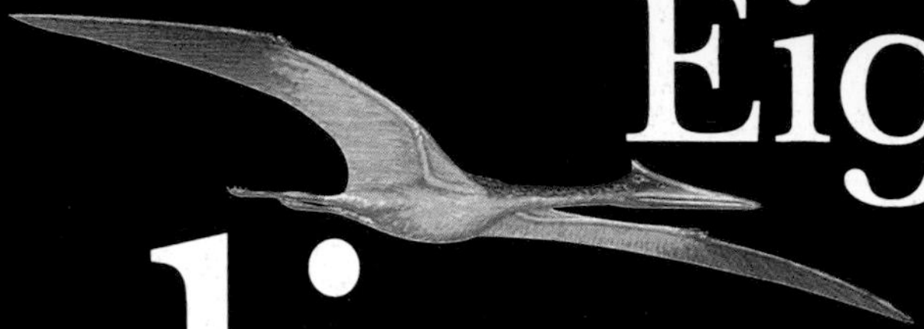

Eight

dinosaurs

by

Kate Petty

Illustrated by
James Field,
Mike Lacy, and Jo Moore

Introduction

Discover for yourself amazing facts about prehistoric life, how big the animals were, what they ate, how they had babies, and how we know all this.

Did *you* know that dinosurs died out 65 million years ago? ... dinosaur means "terrible lizard?" ... some dinosaurs were bigger than a four-story building? ... some dinosaurs hunted in packs? ... most dinosaurs ate plants? ... dinosaurs laid eggs? ... some dinosaurs were armor-plated? ... some dinosaurs had head-butting contests? ... *Quetzalcoatlus* was bigger than a hang glider? ... there were real sea monsters in dinosaur times? ... some dinosaurs had feathers?

I didn't know that

all the dinosaurs died out 65 million years ago. For 150 million years earth was a planet inhabited by dinosaurs until disaster struck – maybe a meteorite hit the earth or maybe a large number of volcanoes erupted – and the dinosaurs were no more.

We know about dinosaurs because people have discovered their fossilized remains in rocks. Fossil specialists, or paleontologists, can piece them together and work out how they lived.

True or false?
Humans were responsible for making the dinosaurs extinct.

Answer: **False**
Humans and dinosaurs never lived together on earth. Over 60 million years separate the last dinosaurs and our earliest ancestors.

One Million Years B.C. – the film that got it wrong!

Saltasaurus

Dinosaur history is divided into three periods: Triassic (early), Jurassic (middle), and Cretaceous (late). Different dinosaurs lived in different periods.

Coelophysis

Tyrannosaurus

Stegosaurus

Cretaceous

Jurassic

Triassic

! Crocodiles have hardly changed at all since dinosaur times.

One of the differences between dinosaurs and other reptile families, such as crocodiles or lizards, is that dinosaurs walked on straight legs.

A dinosaur's skin would have been very tough and scaly to the touch. Like a snake's skin, which people sometimes expect to be slimy, it would in fact have felt dry and bumpy.

Close-up of
T. rex's skin

I didn't know that

dinosaur means "terrible lizard." By 1841 people realized that these enormous fossilized bones belonged to huge extinct reptiles, not giant humans! A scientist named Dr. Richard Owen named them "dino" (terrible) "saurs" (lizards).

Tyrannosaurus rex

Thirty-nine feet tall with a three-foot-wide mouth and teeth as long as carving knives, *Tyrannosaurus rex* was a nightmare lizard! Its name means King Tyrant Lizard.

T. rex's fossilized tooth

The first dinosaur discovered in the West was in 1824.

I didn't know that some dinosaurs were bigger than a four-story building. *Ultrasauros* was a huge *sauropod*, the biggest dinosaur ever, at 98 feet long and 39 feet high. A human would barely have reached its ankles!

Compsognathus

SEARCH & FIND
Can you find nine Compsognathuses?
FIND & SEARCH

Ultrasauros

Fossilized footprints show that these enormous sauropods moved in groups, walking with long strides. Some might have swum across rivers, pulling themselves along with their front legs.

The chicken-sized *Compsognathus* was one of the smallest dinosaurs. It was a speedy meat-eater, which chased after tiny mammals, lizards, and insects.

! *Mamenchisaurus* had a 33-foot-long neck!

Deinocheirus

A hug from *Deinocheirus*, "terrible hand," would have been deadly! Its arms were over eight feet long. This birdlike creature was probably bigger than *T. rex*.

Tenontosaurus

All meat-eating dinosaurs were *theropods*, with three toes and long claws. Most walked on two legs.

SEARCH & FIND SEARCH & FIND

Can you find the *Tenontosaurus* that got away?

Deinonychus

I didn't know that

some dinosaurs hunted in packs. Fossils have been found of a group of *Deinonychuses* surrounding a *Tenontosaurus*, a *herbivore*. They probably hunted it together like lions or wolves do today.

Deinonychus had long claws for stabbing and cutting. On each hind foot it had a special slashing claw, which could be pulled back when it ran.

157

Sauropods (like Diplodocus and Apatosaurus) had teeth like pegs for raking leaves or spoon-shaped ones for pulling leaves off a plant. They swallowed without chewing.

Apatosaurus

I didn't know that

most dinosaurs ate plants.

The earliest dinosaurs were meat-eaters, but by the Jurassic period plant-eaters were flourishing. There was still no grass to graze on – instead they grazed on other plants.

Big plant-eating dinosaurs had to eat 400 pounds of leaves a day!

Scientists can also learn about dinosaur diets from their fossilized droppings, which might contain seeds, leaves, or fish scales.

Hadrosaurs (duckbills like *Parasaurolophus* and *Edmontosaurus*) could eat Christmas trees! They ground twigs and pine needles between jaws that contained more than a thousand teeth, pressed together into ridged plates.

Centrosaurus

Edmontosaurus

Ceratopsian dinosaurs (like *Centrosaurus*) had parrotlike beaks for cropping very tough plants, with strong jaws and sharp teeth for cutting them up.

I didn't know that

dinosaurs laid eggs. They did – just like all reptiles. The dinosaur mother would scrape out a hollow nest in the ground and cover the eggs to keep them warm. She would bring food to her babies until they could leave the nest.

True or false?

The biggest dinosaurs laid giant eggs three feet long.

Answer: **False**

Even the biggest dinosaur eggs were no more than five times the size of a chicken's egg. A bigger egg would need to have a thicker shell. This would suffocate the baby.

SEARCH & FIND & SEARCH & FIND &

Can you find the imposter?

Maiasaura

Fossilized footprints of small tracks surrounded by larger ones show that young dinosaurs on the move were protected by the older, larger ones.

Like a cuckoo, the *Troodon* may have laid its eggs in others' nests.

Carnotaurus

I didn't know that

some dinosaurs were armor-plated. This was protection from the fierce meat-eaters such as *Carnotaurus* that hunted them. Like armadillos and porcupines today, certain plant-eaters had tough skins or spikes.

Euoplocephalus

Euoplocephalus even had bony eyelids! It also had spikes and a lethal clubbed tail for defense – enough to make any predator think twice.

Sauropods were protected by sheer size, but a group of *Triceratops* could make a wall of horns that would scare off their enemies.

Tyrannosaurus rex

Triceratops

True or false?
The spiny plates on a *Stegosaurus* were for protection.

Answer: **False**

They were probably for controlling its body heat. Blood so near the skin's surface could warm up very quickly in the Sun or cool down in the shade.

Diplodocus used its tail as a defensive whip.

I didn't know that

some dinosaurs had head-butting contests. Like rams and stags today, "*boneheads*" such as *Stegoceras* battled for leadership. Their skulls were 10 inches thick, so it probably didn't hurt too much.

Parasaurolophus

Stegoceras

Some duck-billed dinosaurs, like *Parasaurolophus,* had hollow headpieces that were connected to their nasal passages. They might have snored! They didn't use their crests for fighting head to head.

SEARCH & FIND
Can you find the chameleon?
FIND & SEARCH

No one knows what colors dinosaurs were. Like reptiles and birds today, they were probably colored to blend in with their surroundings. Like chameleons, some might have changed color.

True or false?
Pterosaurs had feathers.

Answer: **False**

More like bats than birds, pterosaurs like
Dimorphodon had furry bodies and leathery
wings. They had beaked faces,
but they also had teeth.

Dimorphodon

Rhamphorynchus

I didn't know that

Quetzalcoatlus was bigger than
a hang glider. With a wingspan of
32 feet, it was the biggest creature ever
to take to the air, gliding on warm air
currents. Flying reptiles were not
dinosaurs but *pterosaurs*.

Pteranodon

The winged dinosaur, *Archaeopteryx*, was probably the first bird.

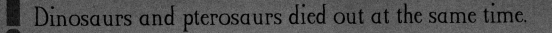

! Dinosaurs and pterosaurs died out at the same time.

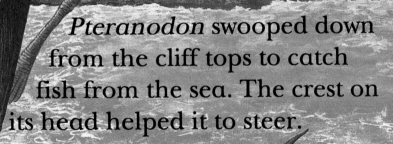

Quetzalcoatlus

Pteranodon swooped down from the cliff tops to catch fish from the sea. The crest on its head helped it to steer.

Pterodaustro also ate fish. It had a sieve in its beak so it could strain tiny fish as it flew low over the water.

I didn't know that

there were real sea monsters in dinosaur times. Dinosaurs didn't live in the sea, but it was full of all sorts of other huge and strange-looking swimming reptiles. They fed on fish and shellfish.

Elasmosaurus

The *plesiosaur Elasmosaurus* was 50 feet long and nearly all neck. Swimming through the water, it must have looked like *Diplodocus* with flippers!

The turtlelike *Archelon* was longer than a rowboat.

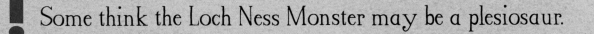

! Some think the Loch Ness Monster may be a plesiosaur.

Ichthyosaurs were some of the earliest sea reptiles. They looked like dolphins and, like them, breathed air. They fed on the *ammonites* and *belemnites* you often find as fossils today.

Ichthyosaurs

Liopleurodon was one of the short-necked plesiosaurs. It really was a monster – its head was seven feet long!

Mosasaurus

Mosasaurs were some of the last sea reptiles and, at 33 feet long, the largest lizards ever. They looked like dragons, but with flippers rather than legs.

Liopleurodon

Paleontologists piece together dinosaur bones into skeletons. Then they flesh out the skeletons. They have to guess the colors. Take your own dinosaur models and paint them. What colors will you choose and why?

I didn't know that

some dinosaurs had feathers.

A fossil of a feathered dinosaur was found in China in 1996. New discoveries can change the way we think about dinosaurs. Just imagine how different they would look with feathers!

Close-up view of feathers

You will never be able to see moving, living dinosaurs in a zoo. But there are many exhibitions of lifelike, moving dinosaurs all over the world. Try to find the one nearest to you. Write to them for information and visit it if you can.

Even though the feathers were probably for warmth rather than for flying, this find makes it even more likely that modern birds are related to dinosaurs.

If you can't visit any moving dinosaurs you can see them at the movies.

Chapter Nine

birds & bugs

by Claire Llewellyn

Illustrated by
Chris Shields, Myke Taylor,
Rob Shone, and
Jo Moore

Introduction

Discover for yourself amazing facts about some of the many different types of bugs and birds.

Find out how they walk, crawl, and fly, what they eat, how they catch their food, and how they eat it. Also discover what various types of bugs and birds look like, and how they defend themselves.

Did *you* know that insects have six legs? ... some insects eat lizards? ... a stick insect is the bigget insect in the world? ... all birds have feathers? ... some birds hang upside down? ... some flocks contain a million birds?

I didn't know that

insects have six legs. Beetles, ants, and all other insects have three pairs of legs. Counting the legs is a sure way of identifying an insect. Woodlice, spiders, mites, and centipedes aren't insects – they have far too many legs.

An insect has three different parts to its body: the head, the *thorax*, and the *abdomen*. A hard outer skeleton makes the insect waterproof and protects its soft insides.

Goliath beetle

Eye Brain Thorax Stomach

Abdomen

Woodlouse

Heart

Mouth Leg

The first insects lived 370 million years ago – long before the dinosaurs.

SEARCH & FIND ◆ FIND ◆ SEARCH & FIND ◆ SEARCH

Find one insect and three imposters.

People who study insects are called entomologists. They learn about insects, how and where they live, and how best to protect them.

Centipede

Bird-eating spider

There are well over a million kinds of insects in the world. That's more than all the other kinds of animals put together! Entomologists discover 8,000 new insects every year.

175

I didn't know that

some insects eat lizards.

When a praying mantis snaps its spiny legs, its helpless prey is trapped inside. Mantises are fierce hunters. Most of them eat other insects, but some catch lizards and frogs.

Praying mantis

A female mantis is so dangerous, she'll even eat her mate.

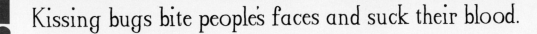

SEARCH & FIND & SEARCH & FIND
Can you find the praying mantis' meal?

Some tropical moths feed on the salty tears of horses and deer. The moths flutter around the animals' eyes to make them cry!

Mosquito

When the assassin bug catches a tasty meal, it injects it with poison. This turns the prey's body to soup. Then the bug sucks it all up.

Not all mosquitoes suck blood – only the females do. They need blood to make their eggs. Male mosquitoes feed on nectar.

Assassin bug

Five hundred years ago, rat fleas were the most dangerous insects in the world. They spread a deadly sickness called the plague, which killed millions and millions of people.

When the Queen Alexandra birdwing butterfly spreads its wings, it measures 11 inches (28 cm) from wingtip to wingtip. No wonder it's mistaken for a bird.

! Fleas can jump an incredible 130 times their own height.

I didn't know that

a stick insect is the biggest insect in the world. The Indonesian giant stick insect measures more than 12 inches from head to toe. It's so big that it moves very slowly.

SEARCH & FIND
Can you find ten fairy flies?
FIND & SEARCH

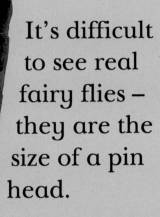

It's difficult to see real fairy flies – they are the size of a pin head.

Male cicadas are the loudest insects in the world. Their clicking noise can be heard by females half a mile away.

I didn't know that

all birds have feathers. Birds are the only animals that have feathers. Feathers keep birds warm and help them to fly. Dull feathers may hide a bird. Colorful ones help to attract a mate.

Peacock

There is an Arabian legend about a magical bird called the phoenix. Every 500 years, the phoenix is said to set itself on fire and is born again from the ashes.

True or false?
Birds are the only animals
that can fly.

Fruit bat

Answer: **False**

Insects, such as bees and butterflies, fly
through the air on fine gauzy wings.
Bats can also fly. They are mammals,
and their wings are covered with
thin sheets of skin.

Scientists who
study birds are
called
ornithologists.
They learn all about birds and the
way they behave. But many people
are interested in birds and become
eager and expert bird-watchers.

! The kiwi can't fly. Its feathers are soft and hairy.

I didn't know that

some birds hang upside down. During the breeding season, male birds of paradise hang upside down from a branch to show off their beautiful feathers. They try to look their best to attract the attention of a mate.

Japanese cranes dance with each other in the breeding season. They wave their heads up and down, raise and flap their wings, and make funny leaps up in the air.

Blue bird of paradise

Male and female swans stay with their mates for life.

A male frigate bird shows off by blowing up a big red pouch on its neck.

A male bald eagle dazzles his mate with a fantastic flying display. He swoops through the air, making daredevil dives at up to 100 mph.

SEARCH & FIND

Can you find five butterflies?

True or false?
Birds sing to attract a mate.

Answer: **True**
Some of the top singers, such as this banded pitta, like to stay hidden in bushes and trees. Singing out loud is a good way for a male to get himself noticed. And it tells other males to keep off his nest.

183

True or false?
Some birds fly as fast as an
express train.

Peregrine falcon

Answer: **True**

The peregrine falcon is the fastest bird in the world. It
attacks other birds in midair by diving down on to them
at speeds of nearly 170 mph.

Ostrich

The ostrich is the
world's biggest bird. It grows up to nine
feet tall. The Cuban bee hummingbird is
the smallest bird in the world – it is no bigger
than a bee.

Red-billed quelea

The bee hummingbird can even fly backward.

I didn't know that

some flocks contain a million birds. The red-billed quelea lives in Africa in huge flocks of millions of birds. They feed on grass seeds, and can ruin a farm crop in minutes – just like a swarm of locusts.

The bird with the longest beak is the Australian pelican. Its scissorlike bill grows up to 18.5 inches long, and must be very useful when preening!

Glossary

Abdomen
The last of the three parts of an insect's body.

Ammonites
Prehistoric shellfish, commonly found as fossils.

Arachnid
An animal, such as the spider, that has 8 legs.

Baleen
"Baleen" whales are toothless whales. Baleen is the name given to the horny plates that hang down from the roof of a toothless whale's mouth for filtering its food.

Belemnites
Prehistoric bullet-shaped shellfish, also common fossils.

Blowhole
The whale's nostril on top of its head.

Blubber
The thick layer of fat that lies under the skin of animals such as whales and keeps out the cold.

Boneheads
The nickname given to Pachycephalosaurs. They were two-legged dinosaurs with very, very thick skulls.

Camouflage
The colors and markings on an animal that help it to blend in with its surroundings.

Cartilage
The material that forms the skeletons of sharks and rays.

Ceratopsians
Dinosaurs that had horns and a protective bony frill.

Cold-blooded
Animals that take their heat from the temperature outside are cold-blooded.

Crocodilian
The ancient reptile family which includes

crocodiles, alligators, caimans, and gavials.

Crustacean
An animal, such as a lobster or a crab, that has a hard outer shell and lots of legs.

Display
The way that animals show off to each other, such as when a peacock spreads its tail feathers.

Exoskeleton
The hard outer covering that protects the body of spiders and many other animals.

Food chain
A food chain shows the feeding links between living things. Each "link" in a food chain is eaten by the next. Such as, grass is eaten by zebras, which are eaten by lions.

Fossil
Animal remains that have turned to stone over millions of years.

Hadrosaurs
Duck-billed dinosaurs, often with a crest on their head.

Hatchling
An animal that has just come out of its egg.

Herbivore
A plant-eater.

Hibernate
To spend the winter in a kind of deep sleep.

Ice Age
Periods between two million and 10,000 years ago, when ice sheets sometimes covered large parts of the earth.

Ichthyosaurs
Dolphin-like sea reptiles that lived at the same time as dinosaurs.

Insect
A creature with six legs and three parts to its body.

Ligament
A ligament is like a strap. It is made of tough material that holds bones in place at the joints.

Mammal
An animal, such as a cat, that gives birth to its young and nourishes it with milk.

Glossary

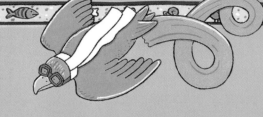

Migrate
To make journeys in search of food or warmth.

Mosasaurs
Dragonlike sea reptiles that lived at the same time as dinosaurs.

Nocturnal
Out and about at night.

Organ
Any part of the body that has a special purpose, such as the eyes that are the organs of sight and the ears that are the organs of hearing.

Paleontologists
Scientists that study the fossilized remains of extinct animals and plants.

Parasites
Animals that live on other animals (known as hosts) and get food from them. A parasite always damages its host.

Plankton
Microscopic plants and animals that live in the sea.

Plesiosaurs
Sea reptiles with flippers rather than legs, that lived at the same time as dinosaurs.

Pod
A small group of animals, especially whales or seals.

Predator
An animal that kills and eats other animals.

Prehistoric
The time long ago before there were any written records.

Primate
A member of the primate family, which includes humans, apes, and monkeys.

Pterosaurs

A group of flying reptiles that lived at the same time as dinosaurs.

Reptile

The animal family to which snakes, crocodiles, and dinosaurs all belong.

Sauropods

A group of long-necked, long-tailed, four-legged, plant-eating dinosaurs.

School

The name for a large group of sea animals.

Shoal

A large group or school of fish.

Streamlined

Having a smooth body shape that moves easily through the water.

Tapetum

The shiny part at the back of a cat's eye that helps it to see in the dark.

Territory

An area of land which an animal treats as its own and defends against other animals.

Theropods

A group of meat-eating dinosaurs. Most of them walked on two legs.

Thorax

The middle part of an insect's body, between the head and the abdomen.

Warm-blooded

Warm-blooded creatures make warmth inside their bodies. Cold-blooded creatures are warm or cold according to the temperature outside.

Windpipe

The tube in the body that is an air passage between the mouth and the lungs.

Index

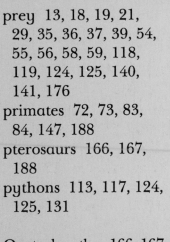

Index